The A
of Clu

Jean-Denis Salvèque, *administrator of the abbey, president of the Centre d'études clunisiennes*

The Benedictine monks of Baume-les-Messieurs and Gigny (Franche-Comté) settled at Cluny in the 10th century. At that time no one could imagine that, less than two hundred years later, Cluny would be a unique monastic capital, playing a leading spiritual and economic role. The heart of Western monasticism and market-town attesting to the revival of urban life, Cluny offered one of the most successful models of Romanesque culture, promoting peace and benevolence. Rebuilt and embellished several times, the site bears witness to more than one thousand years of a rich history whose major events were at the scale of the Western world. "It is said that Cluny is as majestic as the ruins of ancient Rome": the monks have since been gone for over two hundred years,

and ordinary life has reclaimed its rights. Yet if Cluny's splendour has become immaterial, its message still remains everpresent.

The founding of the abbey

Previous double page
Aerial view of the abbatial site, looking south-east.

Right page
Cluny, seen from the north, circa 1670, engraving by Louis Prévost, detail (Paris, Bibliothèque nationale de France).

♦***Villa:*** *The central buildings of a farmstead under the Roman empire.*

Located in southern Burgundy, Cluny nestles in a small, north-south oriented valley drained by the Grosne River, a tributary of the Saône. The region of Cluny covers an area extending 15 kilometres from the Saône-Rhône axis. It is covered by shrubs and woodland up to the slopes of the highest hills, with their forest-clad rounded forms. While some sandstone or granitic outcrops can be perceived on the summits, the cultivated limestone slopes provide excellent and abundant building materials.

Burgundy is a region of transit and encounters: for thousands of years people and merchandise, ideas and innovations passed though this province. Many traces of prehistoric times are still clearly visible, in particular megaliths. Several Gallo-Roman *villae*♦ are known to have existed in the immediate vicinity of Cluny. Many of the administrative structures of Late Antiquity outlived the Roman empire, and the region was inhabited throughout the early Middle Ages. Dwellings were grouped to form hamlets, then villages, around the *villae*.

Arms of the abbey, vault of Jean de Bourbon's chapel: Saint Peter's keys and Saint Paul's sword.

The earliest written testimony of human settlement on the site of the future abbey dates from the 9th century. It was thus a well-organised and cultivated locality which welcomed the new monastic community as the year 1000 approached. Guillaume, Duke of Aquitaine, called the Pious, Count of Mâcon and Bourges by God's graces, proposed to Bernon, abbot of Baume-les-Messieurs and Gigny, to found a house of prayer on one of his estates. On 11 September 910, he signed the foundation act in his hometown of Bourges. Twelve monks took up residence on the rural domain of the Cluny *villa*. Placed under the protection of Saints Peter and Paul, they followed Saint Benedict's rule. Guillaume renounced all rights over the new foundation: only the Holy See was to be suzerain there. This independence, reinforced in 998 by the confirmation of its exemption♦, safeguarded the abbey from secular authorities (for example, the Bishop of Mâcon) and was the key to Cluniac success.

♦***Exemption:*** *A provision emanating from the Holy See in Rome allowing a monastery to benefit from special derogations.*

Cluny 1

Devoutness and humility

11th-century capital, Romanesque cloister at Cluny.

The monks of Cluny were free to choose their abbot. Several men of outstanding merit succeeded one another: Odon (927-942), an exceptional intellect and writer, and later Mayeul (963-994), born into the Provence aristocracy, established solid foundations which made it a model monastery. Because of the right of reform granted by Pope John XI in 932, the abbot of Cluny could agree to direct any other monastery wishing to follow his precepts. The Burgundian abbey's spiritual influence grew, especially with the arrival of Abbot Odilon de Mercœur (994-1049) in Auvergne. The network, including over 800 abbeys and priories distributed throughout Europe - as far away as Poland - represented a major constituent of Christendom.

The abbot exercised remarkable political influence over sovereigns and played an increasingly important role as arbitrator. Odilon shrewdly bestowed an important position on his abbey in the organisation of feudal authority. Lords and warriors, encouraged to practise a moral way of life suited to lay people, were under obligation to provide the abbey with land and churches. Socially, chivalry fulfilled a religious function. Odilon participated in establishing the "Truce of God" which forbade all violence from Wednesday evenings to Monday mornings, in order to oblige the powerful to respect the life and property of those who were not entitled to make war, such as peasants, clergy and the weak.

Abbot Odilon de Mercœur, reliquary, painted wood, 15th century (Souvigny, abbey church).

Divine Office (a permanent dialogue with heaven) played a leading role at Cluny. Devotion to the dead was magnified: all those who associated themselves, through donations, with the great Cluniac family benefitted from perpetual prayers by the monks for the eternal repose of their souls. Gradually, whole dynasties of donors were formed. In order to mark this intercession formally, around 1030 Odilon inaugurated All Souls' Day on 2 November, still celebrated in our times. Countless vocations swelled the number of *profès*, or those taking religious vows.

Worship and rites

Cluniac monks, perhaps more than any others, were committed to developing a taste for grandiose ceremonies. Gold, incense and songs were part of their daily life; the arts, and above all that of building, were consecrated to the service of the Divine Office. The cult of saints rapidly played an important role, in particular that of Saints Peter and Paul, patrons of the abbey, but also John the Evangelist, Mary Magdalene, the Virgin Mary and Saints Marcel, Martin and James, became objects of great devotion. The saintly abbots of Cluny were also venerated: Odon, Mayeul, Odilon, and the greatest of all, Hugues. Prayers were addressed to all these saints, protectors of the monastery, imploring their intercession with God. The cult of relics was particularly developed; inventories enumerate an impressive list. The Cluniac monks encouraged pilgrimages for lay people without actually initiating them, the most famous being that to the shrine of Saint James at Compostela. They maintained a prudent attitude concerning the crusades.

By serving God in humility and poverty, monks were more certain to attain celestial Jerusalem. Above all else, they were men of prayer and meditation, their lives marked by numerous canonical services: nocturns or vigils between 1.30 and 3 a.m. depending on the season, matins between 3.30 and 5 a.m., followed by daily prime, tierce, sext, nones, vespers and compline.

The "Cluny lectionary", Cluniac illumination: Pentecost (Paris, Bibliothèque nationale de France).

Cluny 2

A model monastery

Chevet:
The apsidal end of a church, sometimes with an attached group of apses.

Galilee:
A vestibule, or occasionally a chapel, situated in the western section of religious buildings.

In 981 the abbey inaugurated a particularly elaborate monastic building complex. The new abbey church included a chevet♦ extending around a straight bay leading to a large apse and staggered chapels. A projecting transept, crowned by a tall belfry, was preceded by a nave, a porch called a "galilee"♦ and an atrium. This plan was to serve as a model for many contemporary churches. The cloister and monastic buildings extended to the south of the nave, thus profitting from a favourable exposure.

Established just outside the monastery gates, the lay community developed and participated in the prosperous economic context generated by the growing number of visitors. The abbot imposed himself as its lord and exercised rights of justice over its members.

Cluny and the monastery buildings, circa 1043, drawing by Kenneth John Conant (Cluny, Musée d'Art et d'Archéologie-Musée Ochier).

In 1049 Odilon's long abbacy ended. A very young abbot, Hugues de Semur, born into an aristocratic family from Brionne, was then appointed. For sixty years he pursued his predecessors' work, increasing the institution's prestige and authority. A great builder, Hugues undertook the enlargement of most of the monastic buildings and, at the age of sixty-four, launched the construction of a new abbey church.

Gunzo's dream

During the abbacy of Hugues de Semur, Gunzo, an old and bedridden monk, had a dream: he saw Saint Peter, Saint Paul and Saint Stephen placing markers as indicators of a new sanctuary site at Cluny. They told him that he had to convince his father abbot of the need to build a new abbey church, as the one consecrated in 981 had become too small for the large number of monks. To everyone's surprise, on the very next day Gunzo left his bed and went to report his vision to the abbot who was meeting with the community in the chapter house. He succeeded in persuading him to launch a great new building project to the north of Cluny 2. Abbot Hugues probably would have needed this intervention to convince his monks, very certainly reticent to abandon their church to which they were deeply attached.

The vision of monk Gunzo: Saints Peter, Paul and Stephen indicate the plans of the future abbey church, Cluny 3; Gunzo relates his vision to Abbot Hugues. Manuscript n° 135 of Saint-Martin-des-Champs (Paris, Bibliothèque nationale de France).

beatorum apostolorum Petri et Pauli. Sacra-
uit etiam ipse et altare sedem
misse matutinalis. Lugdunen-
sis autem archiepiscopus hugo. Pisanus
archiepiscopus dalbertus: Episcopus signinus
bruno. eodem die in ipso monas-
terio iubente papa tria in tribus
primis cancellis sacrarunt alta-
ria. Tunc papa inter faciendo mis-
sasque agendo. post alia salutis hor-
tamenta. coram episcopis et cardinalibus
multorumque personis. huiuscemodi
sermonem habuit ad populum.

Pope Urban II's consecration of an altar at Cluny 3, 25 October 1095. On the right, facing the apse, Abbot Hugues, with mitre and crosier, is surrounded by his monks. To the left of the baldachin, the pope blesses the altar. As the key figure in the scene, he is the only person whose feet intrude onto the base line. Manuscript n° 135 of Saint-Martin-des-Champs (Paris, Bibliothèque nationale de France).

Cluny 3

The "angels' parvis♦"

This church, also called the *maior ecclesia*, can rightfully be considered a masterpiece of classical Romanesque art and the high point of Cluniac art. Built at approximately the same time as Saint-Sernin in Toulouse and Santiago de Compostela, this huge edifice - the largest church in the whole of Christendom until Saint Peter's Cathedral was rebuilt in Rome in the 16th century - was the outcome of the efforts of several generations of Romanesque builders.

♦Parvis: *The open space in front of a church; probably a corruption of paradisus.*

It was a skilful combination of a highly developed central-plan building (apse, choir bay, small transept) with a basilica-plan type (several naves) linked by a large transept, where both Eastern and Western

Reconstruction of Cluny 3, drawing by Jean-Claude Barat (Nevers, Bibliothèque municipale).

influences are perceptible (Santa Sophia, Constantinople, and Saint Peter's, Rome). Richly embellished with 1,200 capitals and murals, its vaulted interior was flooded with a soft light. Admirably distributed, this lighting accentuated the effect of soaring height (the main nave rose 30 metres above floor level) through the multiplication of windows at the springing point of the vaults.

The liturgy was a major feature in the monk's day. Its development at Cluny was quite exceptional. The Cluniac monks considered praising God in such a setting to be preparation for the hereafter, believing the monastery to be "the celestial Jerusalem" and the *maior ecclesia*, the "angels' parvis". Cluniac authority was then at its height.

Left page **The nave of Cluny 3,** computer reconstruction, TV-All.

Cluny, east view, engraving by Masquelier after a drawing by Jean-Baptiste Lallemand, 18th century (Cluny, Musée d'Art et d'Archéologie-Musée Ochier).

Designated as a second Rome, Cluny was indeed a sort of capital; its renown attracted visitors, both lowly and powerful, from every province.

By associating itself with the decisive reform undertaken by Pope Gregory VII (1073-1085) aimed at restoring discipline and religious spirit within the Latin church, Cluny became a pillar of a move-

West façade of Cluny 3: the two Barabans towers frame the portal of the antechurch and great rose window, drawing by Jean-Baptiste Lallemand, 18th century (Cluny, Musée d'Art et d'Archéologie-Musée Ochier).

ment known as Gregorian reform. This reinstatement of papal supremacy over the appointment of bishops and abbots clarified spiritual and temporal responsibilities. Such reform abolished the practice of simony by certain members of the clergy who, having purchased their office, did not hesitate to make people pay for ministry-related acts. The role played by the abbot of Cluny with the Holy See during the Investiture Conflict, opposing Pope Gregory VII and the German Emperor Henry IV, is indicative of this influence. Wishing to regain control in order to bring greater morality to the Church, the Pope contested the appointment of bishops, invested directly by the emperor with their pastoral mission.

Clunian-style Romanesque wall painting at Berzé-la-Ville, deanery chapel.

The great Cluniac family continued to grow. Prestigious abbeys became its dependants. Five, among the most important, were called "daughter-houses of Cluny": La Charité-sur-Loire, Souvigny, Sauxillanges, Saint-Martin-des-Champs in Paris and

Cluny "denier" coin bearing the inscriptions « PETRUS ET PAULUS » and « CLUNIACO CENEBIO », 12th century.

Town and agricultural possessions

The abbey had close links with the monastic town, on the one hand, and with a series of agricultural possessions (regrouped into granges and deaneries), churches and chapels, on the other. Visiting Cluny without considering these two aspects would give a mistaken idea of its organisation. Extending south and west of the abbey enclosure, the town was in charge of the great abbey gates, thus establishing their interdependence.

From a very early date, the town's inhabitants provided part of the manpower necessary to the organisation of the monastery and activities related to building erection and maintenance. Profitting from financial benefits derived from the many visitors to Cluny, as well as tributes and taxes received or levied, they soon engaged in monetary transactions. The town, where the Lord-Abbot exercised the right of justice, was placed under the responsibility of a provost, a rich and influential personage. A fortified wall was erected toward the early 12th century.

The monks' agricultural possessions, of which the most important were placed under the supervision of a doyen, or dean, supplied the means necessary for communal subsistence. Wheat, barley and vineyards were cultivated; within a 50-kilometre radius, the availability of fish, pigs, sheep and wood contributed to the abbey's wealth. Dues and rental monies were also collected from these estates. The doyens were placed directly under the authority of the grand prior, the most important "lieutenant" in the Cluniac hierarchy.

Cluniac deanery at Mazille, lower and upper chapels, 13th century.

Affiliated abbeys: La Charité-sur-Loire, the first "daughter-house of Cluny" *(top)* and Moissac *(bottom right)*.

Bottom left **The deanery at Jalogny.**

Saint Pancras at Lewes in England. In all, over 1,100 possessions were spread over ten provinces in the territories of France, Germany, Switzerland, Italy, Spain and Great Britain, including the famous abbeys of Mozac, Moissac, Charlieu and Romainmôtier, to which important deaneries♦ such as Mazille, Jalogny, Bézornay and Berzé-la-Ville must be added.

When Hugues died in 1109, the great abbey church building project had almost reached completion due to some very important donations, in particular the exceptional generosity of the King of Spain, Alfonso VI of Castile.

♦**Deanery:** *An agricultural estate provisioning an abbey.*

Organisation of the Cluniac order

Daily life of Cluniac monks, miniature from the *Miroir historial* by Vincent de Beauvais, 15th century (Chantilly, Musée Condé).

The brief abbacy of Pons de Melgueil left the abbey in disarray. In 1122 the monks elected Pierre de Montboissier, known as Peter the Venerable. This distinguished and charitable man presided over the destiny of Cluny until 1156. Together with Pope Innocent II, it was he who was responsible for consacrating Cluny in 1130.

Right page **Devotion of Cluniac monks to the Virgin Mary,** manuscript n° 135 of Saint-Martin-des-Champs (Paris, Bibliothèque nationale de France).

Meanwhile new ideas were circulating which gave birth to the Cistercian order founded by Saint Bernard, a monastic movement preaching austerity and renunciation of the temporal world. All the abbot of Cluny's moderation and wisdom were required to appease quarrels between monks of the two observances. The debate between Cluniacs and Cistercians was generally confined to scholastic disputes where differences of opinion concerning monastic life seldom entered into consideration.

Peter the Venerable's efforts, however, failed to bring about a return to the energy and enthusiasm of previous centuries. Nine abbots succeeded one another between 1157 and 1209. But it was only in the 13th century, at the beginning of the Gothic period, that the Cluniac family organised into a

♦Visitor: *A monk responsible for supervising the application of the rule in force in the monasteries.*

Peter the Venerable

The personality of Pierre de Montboissier (c. 1094-1156), called Peter the Venerable, is well known because of abundant surviving correspondence. Wise and lucid, he paid great attention to understanding contemporary problems with a judicious mind. He counselled the king of France and enjoyed excellent relations with Abbot Suger of Saint-Denis, although rather more difficult ones with Saint Bernard whom he opposed on the question of the sumptuousness of religious buildings. At Cluny, he sought to return monastic life to a certain austerity which had been forgotten because of success and the accumulation of wealth. His abbacy marked the end of Cluniac expansion.
Montboissier took up the defence of Abelard, eminent authority at the Écoles de Paris and most brilliant intellect of his day, at a time when he was attacked by Saint Bernard and condemned in 1140 by a synod [ecclesiatical court] at Sens. Abelard sought refuge at Cluny and ended his life in the Cluniac abbey of Saint-Marcel-lès-Chalon.
Peter the Venerable sought to acquire and disseminate Arabian scientific learning. He commissioned a Latin translation of the Koran to better combat infidels, not militarily but intellectually.

Page of the Koran, illustrated manuscript (detail), Algeria.

powerful monastic order within the Roman church. Placed under the abbot's direction, a general chapter supervised the order and dispatched visitors♦ from monastery to monastery.

For Cluny, however, the period was not one of expansion. And, despite events shaking the Western world - the Hundred Years War, the Great Western Schism (between 1378 and 1417, two rival popes reigned, one in Rome, the other in Avignon) - the abbey enjoyed satisfactory material conditions until the end of the 14th century. Numerous building projects were undertaken: the "Palace of Pope Gelasius", the flour store and cellarage or store-room, as well as the building known as "la Malgouverne".

Cluniacs and Cistercians

Both orders originated in the Rule of Saint Benedict of Nursia, written circa 540 and amended by Saint Benedict of Aniane in 817. Their differences lay in their manner of observing the Rule and in the relationships between each order and the external world.

Monasteries of both orders were built on the same model: a church flanked by a cloister onto which opened a certain number of rooms (refectory, chapter house, library and upper-floor dormitory). However the Cistercian churches, with their severe architecture, did not generally include a bell tower. While Cistercian monasteries (designed after the model of the Abbey of Cîteaux) are set in a "wilderness" far from all human life on barren land difficult to exploit, Cluny tolerated and encouraged the establishment of neighbouring secular communities; in large part they supplied manpower necessary for building operations and day-to-day running of the abbey.

The two orders did not develop in the same manner. Cluny's influence gave rise to numerous affiliations - amongst others, its unification with the important Abbey of Moissac and its numerous dependencies in 1067. Cîteaux, on the other hand, very early set in place a clear policy of foundations, encouraging the establishment of "daughter-houses", strongly ressembling the model elaborated in the parent abbey.

Cistercian abbeys: Le Thoronet *(top)* and **Silvacane** *(bottom)*.

In the 15th century, a remarkable abbot Jean de Bourbon, bishop of Puy-en-Velay, was appointed in 1456. An excellent administrator and cultivated man, he applied himself to restoring discipline within the order (in accordance with the general movement towards reform) and to encouraging the arts. At Cluny itself, he was responsible for the palace bearing his name, close to the great gates, and the funerary chapel built against the south wall of the small transept in the great church. His successor in 1485, Jacques II d'Amboise, had a building bearing his name added to the first palace, intended to house distinguished guests.

Palace named after Pope Gelasius, with its Gothic clerestory.

Hôtel de Cluny, Paris residence of the abbots of Cluny, 16th century, now the Musée national du Moyen Âge-Thermes et Hôtel de Cluny.

Commendam and Wars of Religion

After these two abbacies had inaugurated the form of administration known as "in commendam"♦, confirming the king of France's hold over the abbey and the order, Cluniacs no longer had the means of safeguarding their independence. Encouraged by the right granted by the Concordat of Bologna (1516) for the sovereign to appoint bishops and abbots, François I succeeded in several attempts to bring monastic orders under royal protection and subjection.

During the early years of the 16th century, the gradual fall of the Cluny monastery was precipitated by the nomination at its head of persons who had, most often, never taken monastic vows. They only rarely visited Cluny, preferring to remain near the royal seat of power. Construction of a prestigious Parisian residence, in the immediate vicinity of the ancient Roman baths of Lutetia, was one blatant symbol of this inclination. The powerful Guise family did not scorn the office of Abbot of Cluny which provided them substantial revenues. The Reformation aroused spirits, and the Wars of Religion ruined many monasteries. Looted by the Huguenots in 1563, and again in 1575, the Abbey of Cluny would never truly recover.

Cartouche of Claude de Guise, abbot of Cluny, 1585, south gable of the palace of Jacques d'Amboise.

♦***Commendam:*** *A regime allowing an abbey to be placed under the protection of a prelate who receives its income.*

The Classical period

Reformation and renewal

From 1510 to 1790 Cluny had only sixteen abbots. The most prestigious appointments were those of Armand Jean du Plessis, Cardinal Richelieu (abbot from 1629 to 1642), Armand de Bourbon, Prince de Conti and son of the Prince de Condé (from 1642 to 1654), Jules, Cardinal Mazarin (from 1655), and, lastly, Emmanuel Théodose de la Tour d'Auvergne, Cardinal Bouillon (from 1683). Bouillon's exile to his Cluny and Tournus abbeys remained much-celebrated after his plotting in Rome and condemnation by Louis XIV. Nonetheless, these abbots of high rank did not halt the order's slow decline. Architectural projects undertaken in the 17th century, although of excellent workmanship, were few in number. Richelieu left a monumental doorway, now dismantled, which decorated the entrance to the monastic buildings on the façade bearing the name of Pope Gelasius. Cardinal Bouillon was responsible for some magnificent sculptures, part of the funerary monument he had wished to install in honour of his family, in the northern section of the small transept of the great church, but which was forbidden personally by Louis XIV, irritated by the project's splendour.

Armand Jean du Plessis, Cardinal Richelieu, abbot from 1629 to 1642 *(left)*, Philippe de Champaigne, oil on canvas, 1636 (Chantilly, Musée Condé).

Jules, Cardinal Mazarin, abbot from 1655 to 1661 *(right)*, Pierre Mignard, oil on canvas, 1658-1660 (Chantilly, Musée Condé).

Emmanuel Théodose de la Tour d'Auvergne, Cardinal Bouillon, abbot from 1683 to 1710, anonymous, oil on canvas (Cluny, Hôtel-Dieu).

Richelieu introduced Maurist reform [named after the reformed Benedictine congregation of Saint-Maur, founded in Paris in 1618] into his Burgundian monastery. This return to a stricter cloistered life, given official recognition by Pope Gregory XV in 1621, was also called "Strict Observance". Intended to group

Dominique de La Rochefoucauld, last abbot of Cluny, from 1757 to 1790, French school, 18th century, oil on canvas (Cluny, Musée d'Art et d'Archéologie - Musée Ochier).

the various monastic orders to permit the royal government better control of them, this reform was not accepted by the whole community which remained divided, inhabiting different houses of the order.

In 1747 Frédéric-Jérôme de La Rochefoucauld, a favourite of Louis XV, was appointed to the abbacy. The grand prior♦ Dom Dathose had most of the large, rather decrepit, surviving Medieval monastic buildings demolished in order to rebuild them in the Maurist spirit. A vast, new, rather austere cloister was erected, surrounded by numerous galleries serving the refectory, chapels and monks' cells, behind an harmonious façade. With the chevet of the great church, this façade made up a grandiose composition to the east. La Rochefoucauld died in 1757.
He was succeeded by his nephew Dominique. The "Strict Observance" reform triumphed definitively in 1788. It was probably following this change that a major building and embellishment programme was conceived to the west of the cloister. In 1789 the French Revolution put an end to the religious community and its projects.

♦Grand prior: *In an abbey, the permanent delegate of the abbot and his most important lieutenant.*

Great nave of Cluny 3 watercolour by T. Bannister and R. Roz, after work by Kenneth John Conant.

Cluniac gigantism

By the mid-11th century, all projects undertaken at Cluny bore the mark of gigantism. The scale of the role played by Cluny in the Christian world must certainly have urged Cluniacs to surpass conventional limits. The measurements of Abbot Hugues' hostelry (53 by 15 metres), built around 1095 and, even more so, those of the great church (187 metres long with a 77-metre transept) were exceptional for the Middle Ages. These highly ambitious projects were fully and rapidly executed, with no apparent restrictions.
It is difficult for us to imagine ceremonies like Pope Urban II's dedication of the five choir altars of the great church on 25 October 1095, or Pope Innocent II's ultimate consecration, surrounded by 1,000 monks, exactly 35 years later to the day.

This taste for the colossal, which in other respects corresponded to real needs, accompanied abbatial achievements and actions until the monks' definitive departure in 1791. The same large scale characterised Peter the Venerable's infirmary (64 by 22 metres, with a 25-metre height under the panelled vault), indisputably the largest secular building ever built in the Middle Ages, and the Classical monastery begun around 1750. Its north and east galleries around the new cloister were prolonged to form remarkable vistas, vying with the sanctuary's 187-metre length.

Following double page
Saint Martial's chapel and the small aisle during demolition, drawing by Balthazar Hubert de Saint-Didier, early 19th century (private collection).

The French Revolution

The apse under destruction, circa 1810-1820, lithograph by Lefèvre (Paris, Bibliothèque nationale de France).

The suppression of religious communities was pronounced by a decree of the Constituent Assembly on 13 February 1790, but it was only in 1791 that the last forty monks were expelled and their property confiscated. Relatively few former Cluniac monks were persecuted: ten were nonetheless deported to the Île de Ré, including the grand prior Jean-Baptiste Rollet. A member of the Constituent Assembly, Abbot Dominique de La Rochefoucauld, who openly aired opinions opposed to the vote decided by the Civil Constitution of the

Poster announcing the sale, 1804.

Clergy, emigrated to Germany, where he died in 1800. Church furnishings, as well as all the tombs and mausoleums, were destroyed, damaged or burnt by the Revolutionaries. The sale, properly speaking, of the buildings, divided into four lots, was decreed on 2 *floréal an* VI (21 April 1798) by the State, their owner since 1790, and the whole purchased for a modest sum by three associates from Mâcon: Bâtonnard, Vacher and Genillon.

The future of the monastic complex thus became very uncertain. To compensate for the loss of monastic revenues, steps were taken to integrate the site into the town. The market moved into the Classical cloister, transformed into the town square. Its west arcade became a covered street serving a new urban

The apse in ruins, circa 1815-1819, anonymous drawing (Comte de Rambuteau collection).

axis whose orientation line provoked major demolition work resulting in the quasi-complete destruction of the abbey church which was split between the fifth and sixth bays of the nave. Like that of other important sections, its dismantling continued until 1823 in order to install the French national stud farm, amongst other schemes.

It was only in 1866 that the State, after having regrouped all the remaining monastic buildings, installed a specialised teachers' training college, transformed into a school for foremen in 1891, and into an arts and craft college in 1901.

Excavations and major building works

The dismantling of the abbey, but also and above all urbanization work carried out over remnants of the monastic buildings have rendered the interpretation of archaeological remains particularly difficult. Early in the 20th century, according to Cluny inhabitants who remember that period, the very notion of an abbey had been completely erased from local memory.

In 1928 a first major excavation campaign was undertaken, financed by the Medieval Academy of America which sent a brilliant young archaeologist, Kenneth John Conant, to Cluny. The principal aim of this mission (continuing fairly regularly until 1950) was to find again the plan of the gigantic edifice on the site by uncovering wall and pillar foundations preserved in the rubble. These discoveries and the study of documents have enabled a proposed graphic reconstruction of the abbey church architecture and elucidation of its construction history.

Kenneth John Conant during excavations.

The German bombardment of 11 August 1944 incited authorities to envisage reconstruction work in the sector of the antechurch♦ and the Tour des Fromages, taking into account the clearing of monumental vestiges. However, it was not until the 1980s that new operations aimed at developing the site were planned and executed: immediate restoration work and weather protection of the buildings, then from 1985 onwards, a new visitors' circuit covering land annexed by the town, the abbey courtyards, the antechurch, and the more or less unused, neglected enclosure spaces.

♦Antechurch or forechurch: *An appendix to the west end of a church, resembling a porch or narthex, but several bays deep and usually consisting of nave and aisles.*

In 1988 an important campaign began to clear the former antechurch; it was followed by improvement and restoration of the Passage Galilée and the Cour de la Congrégation. Archaeological excavations have

Roof restoration of the belfry called "Clocher de l'Eau bénite", 1980.

been systematically instigated to accompany building works under the control of the Regional Archaeological Service of the Cultural Affairs Department in Dijon, including: 1991, Passage Galilée; 1992, Cour de la Congrégation; 1993, south arm of the great transept. Numerous chance discoveries (fragments of the chancel screen, the frieze from Abbot Hugues' tomb) have allowed new light to be shed on prior knowledge about the furnishings of Cluny 3.

Investigations are continuing beyond the abbey enclosure in order to study the secular heritage of the town of Cluny and former Cluniac possessions. In addition, the Musée Ochier - now the Musée d'Art et d'Archéologie de Cluny - was modernised in 1992. Historians, art historians and archaeologists regularly pool the results of their respective specialised research and collate their opinions. Much still remains to be done to set the site off to best advantage and, first and foremost, to have it recognised as world heritage.

Excavations of the antechurch at the height of the façade of Cluny 3, directed by the Service régional de l'Archéologie, 1989.

Urbanism

The Romanesque capital, reflection of ancient Rome

Cluny 3: Romanesque portal and attic, watercolour after work done by Kenneth John Conant (Cluny, Musée d'Art et d'Archéologie - Musée Ochier).

From the 12th century onwards, stimulated by the great Cluny 3 building campaign, there appeared a marked trend towards a return to the style of Roman antiquity.

Organization of town and church spaces was structured around several axes of which the two principal ones crossed perpendicularly - that of the great church and that of the most prestigious street in the town, now Rue de la République. Architecture accompanied and added dignity to this urbanism. At the crossing

Romanesque house, n° 25, Rue de la République, street façade.

point of the two axes stood the abbey gateway with its grand doors. It was conceived to face the town as a veritable double-arched Roman gate crowned by an attic storey. Having crossed through the gateway, one was captured by the lower range of the Romanesque abbey-church façade, its majestic portal projecting outwards, an almost perfect reproduction of a triumphal arch. After having followed the perspective of townhouse façades, the visitor thus wended through the structures of successive monumental doors before entering the mighty naves of the sanctuary.

General view of the church and abbey gates, lithograph by Émile Sagot, 1838 (private collection).

Gothic transformations, reflections of feudalism

Gothic compositions which favoured oblique views, with tower elevations and masses, were rapidly adopted at Cluny. For example, in front of the Romanesque façade, an antechurch was added, pierced with a rose-window and preceded by two enormous crenellated towers called the Barabans. The other towers were either raised and equipped with crenellations and merlons♦ (like the Tour des Fromages), or newly built with hourdis♦ and loopholes. Some crenellated ramparts, whose height was increased on several occasions, surrounded the whole complex. Small bridges spanned certain streets, breaking up urban perspectives.

Tour Fabry, watercolour by A. Verdier, 19th century (Paris, MAP, AP).

Embellishments and grand perspectives

Reconstruction of the monastic buildings during the Classical period initiated a new process enhancing the interior perspectives of the church's naves and transepts, prolonging them with those of the cloister and galleries. To this end, the north and east cloister arcades were considerably extended, reaching a length of nearly 125 metres. To the west of these buildings, a project planned just before 1789, but only roughly outlined on the site, completed this organisation by opening the arcade toward the town. The streets, straightened by a realignment scheme, lost their Medieval appearance with the replacement of overhanging eaves by cornices.

♦Merlon: *The solid section of a parapet, between two embrasures or crenellations.*

♦Hourdis: *A projecting wooden gallery crowning a curtain wall or tower.*

The monks and the architect during monastic building construction circa 1750, Cluny antiphonary (Cluny, Musée d'Art et d'Archéologie - Musée Ochier).

♦**Forum:** *A public square in ancient Roman towns.*

♦**Cardo** *and* **decumanus:** *The main Roman streets, running respectively north-south and east-west, which crossed at the* forum.

Improvements (results of which still remain the most striking) were conceived by municipal officers and economic partners who replaced the monks after 1798. A new thoroughfare was created, at right angles to the main street of Cluny, which meandered south of the abbey enclosure. It served the cloister, which thus became, as in Roman urbanism, a veritable *forum*♦. Mid-18th-century archaeological discoveries at Pompeii may perhaps have inspired the town planners who, in opening up this new thoroughfare, implemented the ancient Roman grid system of the *cardo* and *decumanus*♦.

Main street through Cluny. Façades dating from the Classical period are crowned by cornices.

Visit

The great gates, 12th century.

The great gates[1]

Reached by a small square leading from the Rue de la République (formerly Rue de l'Abbaye), this 12th-century double gate formed the west front of a Romanesque gateway. The two transverse vaulted passages gave access, to the north, to the abbey palaces and garden and, to the south, to the great abbey church. The architectural composition was inspired by great Roman city gates, two of which can be seen at Autun. Despite damage inflicted, it has retained a double access, unique for the Middle Ages. Two grand semicircular arches, confined by fluted pilasters, were probably crowned with an attic storey (a Romantic period drawing suggests a possible reconstruction, see p. 34). Design details and sculptural execution convey extreme refinement. The Corinthian capitals, inherited from the composite Roman order, are set on columns with twisted and straight fluting, reversed from one bay to the next. The Romanesque gateway had been raised in the 16th century by the addition of a pavilion (called "Pavillon de Guise"), pierced with numerous mullion and transom windows and covered by a vast, steeply-pitched hipped roof. Demolitions carried out in 1797 spared only the two gates. Documentary photographs taken around 1880 still show wooden folding doors in one opening, as well as the ground level of the square before excavation.

Fortified enclosure

The Romanesque gateway, while not a projecting construction, marked a strong point in the abbey fencing. Probably late-11th century, built in stone, the enclosure is punctuated by several towers, delimiting an area of about 15 hectares [approximately 37 acres]; it may have replaced a wooden palisade. The wall was laid out with regular stone courses and crowned with crenellations and merlons; its height was increased during several campaigns. Facing the town, it rose to 15 metres which did not prevent inhabitants from building houses against it from the Romanesque period, notably in the vicinity of the gateway.

The round tower[20] commands attention from afar, whether visitors arrive from Mâcon or from Buxy. Set to the north-east of the enclosure, its 30-metre circular form rises straight up to a shallow sloping roof, dominating the surrounding meadows. Several superimposed rooms (the first two in the lower section are vaulted) are serviced by a spiral

staircase housed in a volume adjoined to the main cylindrical building. The top level of the tower, originally defended by a permanent wooden hourdis, is reached by a flight of stairs cut into the thickness of the rampart. Various architectural details, together with the second-storey chimneypiece and recent studies, allow the tower to be dated from 1220.

The Tour Fabry[21] bears the name of Abbot Hugues de Fabry (serving from 1350-1351). Built on the northern flank of the enclosure, it defended the Porte des Prés, a little further to the east, which has now disappeared. Also circular, it dated from the 14th century and was equipped, in the 15th century, with machicolations♦ and a pointed "pepper-pot" roof. Its elegant silhouette, comparable with archetypal fortified castle towers, somewhat helps to disguise its imposing dimensions.

The Tour des Fromages [Cheese Tower][18], formerly called Tour des Fèves [Bean Tower], is the oldest building still standing in the entire abbey. Its lower, slightly sunken, square-plan portion dates from the early 11th century. Its Romanesque masonry ends a few courses of stones above the two small semicircular window bays which mark each wall half-way up. Its height was raised in the 13th century and crenellation gave it a haughty aspect until, during the Age of Enlightenment, it was capped with a pyramidal roof. Marking the southern side of the enclosure, its silhouette is clearly visible from the main street of the town. The tower height was probably increased at the same time as the building known as "la Malgouverne" (now almost totally ruined) was erected against its southern face.

The Tour du Moulin [Mill Tower][22] marks, to the south-east, a change in the direction of the enclosure. This very massive, rectangular-plan tower seems always to have been protected by a roof. It is provided with loopholes on the three sides facing the town, while its interior side, of thinner masonry, is furnished with mullion windows. No doubt its strongest defensive device was a removable wooden hourdis which would only have been installed in case of danger. A spiral staircase gives access to all storeys of the tower which has two latrines overhanging the mill-race♦. The mill (to which the tower owes its name) was housed in the lower room through which flowed a branch of the mill-race called "des Quatre Moulins" [Four Mills]. The association of a defensive building with food-producion indicates the importance the latter assumed for people in the Middle Ages.

Tour Fabry, built on the north enclosure side.

Left page
The round tower, 1220.

♦Machicolation:
An opening in the floor between the corbels of a projecting parapet or covered walk on a tower or wall, through which missiles, molten lead or burning oil could be cast on the enemy below.

♦Mill-race:
An artificial branch of a river created to supply power to a wheel or turbine by means of a change in the water level.

Palace of Jean de Bourbon (south façade) and parvis of Cluny 3.

Palace of Jean de Bourbon [2]

Before the 15th century, the abbots occupied a Romanesque edifice called the "palace of Pope Gelasius", built in front of the atrium of Cluny 2 and enlarged during the Gothic period. Abbot Jean de Bourbon preferred to have an independent residence, directly accessible from the great gates, erected on a plot of ground that he acquired from the monks. This monumental complex included all that was indispensable to the life of a rich prelate: guard room, state and private apartments, kitchens, cloister and chapel. The vast suites of intercommunicating rooms, fitted with magnificent chimneypieces, were served by spiral staircases housed in projecting turrets. In the absence of a monumental entrance characterising secular architectural projects before the 17th century, only the large mullion and transom bays on the first storey of the façade, as well as the gable♦ capping one of them, indicated the high rank of its occupant.

It is probable that the huge roof covered with flat tiles had been decorated with polychrome glazed tiles, common in Burgundy at the end of the Gothic period.

♦***Gable:*** *A pyramidal or gable-shaped canopy over a door or window.*

Palace of Jacques d'Amboise (garden façade) and pavilions, decorated with alabaster plaques.

Palace of Jacques d'Amboise [17]

Doubtless erected by the abbot of the same name, the palace turns its back on the abbey entrance and faces east. Accompanied by a large garden, the refined façade was built at great cost, installed on an imposing retaining wall which compensates for the natural slope of the hill. A central dwelling, originally covered with a hipped roof, is flanked by two elegant pavilions ornamented with alabaster. Constructed, like the main wing, on a substructure with sloping facings, they are embellished on the first level by Gothic tracery♦ and on the second by refined motifs inspired from the Italian Renaissance.
This palace seems to have contained four apartments for high-ranking guests, reached from the rear by a very wide spiral staircase.

♦***Tracery:*** *Ornamental stone openwork in the upper part of a window, screen or panel, or used decoratively in blind arches and vaults.*

Site of Cluny 3: in the foreground, vestiges of the Barabans and antechurch.

The Musée d'Art et d'Archéologie (Musée Ochier)

The museum was installed in 1864 within Jean de Bourbon's palace, following a donation from Jean-Baptiste Ochier's widow to the town of Cluny .

Its lapidary collections, built up from the great capitals of the Cluny 3 choir and the finest sculptural ensembles from the Medieval townhouses, were considerably enriched in the course of excavations carried out by Kenneth John Conant and recent site studies.

Here visitors can discover significant fragments of Romanesque liturgical furnishings from the abbey, in particular vestiges from the Cluny 3 choir screen, various altars and tombs.

Abbot Hugues' funerary monument, which was installed next to the matutinal altar [used for the first daily low Mass], has been well-known since the last discoveries allowing several pieces of its entablature to be reassembled. The ensemble is very homogeneous: fluted pilasters, cornices decorated with palmettes and acanthus leaves, spandrel roses, beading, egg-and-dart pattern and dentils are found throughout the ornamentation, always executed with the same meticulous care.

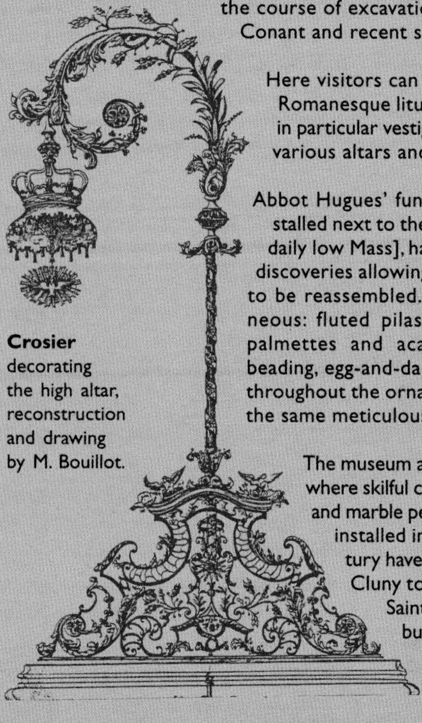

Crosier decorating the high altar, reconstruction and drawing by M. Bouillot.

The museum also houses sections of early paving where skilful compositions combine mosaic work and marble peltae. Choir-stalls with carved backs installed in the abbey choir in the 18th century have unfortunately been removed from Cluny to be refitted into the Cathedral of Saint-Jean's choir in Lyon around 1800, but a gigantic paschal candlestick and a large tabernacle can still be admired in the museum.

Left page
Abbot Hugues' tomb,
watercolour by Alexandre Lenoir (Paris, Musée du Louvre, Département des Arts graphiques).

Choir carpet with the arms of the abbey, perhaps circa 1750 (Cluny, Musée d'Art et d'Archéologie - Musée Ochier).

Altar table and paving from Cluny 3 (details), Romanesque period.

The high altar was embellished with Brother Placide's masterpiece: a frame terminated by a cornice supporting an elegant crosier "where art seems to have depleted delicasy and reunited all that good taste possesses of the richest novel ornaments, rocaille and strokes of fantasy" (B. Dumolin). Nearly 4-metres high, it concealed a mechanical device which allowed a silver dove containing the consecrated host to be raised and lowered. Several fragments of the crosier, destroyed in 1793, were reused in the 1802 tabernacle.

Abbot Hugues' tomb, entablature, reconstruction and drawing by J.-D. Salvèque.

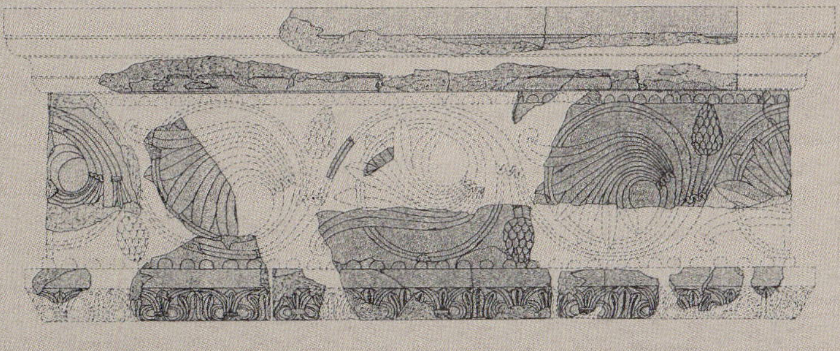

Antechurch, Cluny 3, present arrangement.

Parvis and antechurch[3-4-5]

Shortly after the 1130 dedication, a new programme was launched in front of the Romanesque façade of Cluny 3. Unlike the preceding campaign which only lasted some forty years, this construction work stretched over a long period whose limiting dates are only vaguely known. Projects included the erection of an antechurch with five bays and three naves, and two external towers flanking a narrow façade and broad steps.

The new project had constrained the builders to adapt this extension to the lower contours of the hill bearing Abbot Mayeul's name. Visitors were obliged to descend humbly the 41 steps of this broad staircase punctuated with landings, passing between the two Barabans towers before crossing through the portal of the antechurch.

The Barabans were designed as veritable keeps, austere despite their late 14th-century construction date. Some simple semicircular bays admitted scant light to the rooms which housed the archives (charters, papal bulls and exemptions) in the north tower, and the hall of justice and prisons in the south tower.
The antechurch was built in two, or perhaps three campaigns. It was designed as an immense vestibule used for solemn entries. Its three-storey elevation (four for the two extreme eastern bays) consisted of large arcades, triforium and clerestory. Essentially Romanesque in style, the upper ranges display precocious Gothic forms and structures which southern

Following double page **Romantic reconstruction of the "palace of Pope Gelasius",** with the Richelieu door in place, lithograph by Émile Sagot, 19th century (private collection).

Antechurch, Cluny 3, drawing by Jean-Baptiste Lallemand, 18th century (Paris, Bibliothèque nationale de France).

Frieze from the antechurch (Cluny, Musée d'Art et d'Archéologie - Musée Ochier).

Burgundy was cautiously adopting in the early 13th century. The 25-metre high vaulting, with sharply convex profile, was built on intersecting semicircular arches and was abutted by flying buttresses. Opened on the ground floor by a polychrome portal whose tympanum was replaced by stained glass, its west front was pierced by a sumptuous stone rose-window (10-metre diameter) which admitted west light into the antechurch. Sculpture was generously distributed over the numerous capitals whose modelling, still marked by the last manifestations of the Romanesque style, echoed that of the great pillars.
A delicate carved frieze ornamented the springing line of the triforium just above the arcades. Composed of a series of medallions where roses, fabulous animals and humans alternated, it is, in large part, presented in one of the galleries of the Musée d'Art et d'Archéologie. This west section of the church had been almost completely demolished after 1798 and absorbed into the town. Work begun in 1988 has enabled the ruins to be presented, although the total expanse has not been cleared.
A projection on the ground of the vaulting design and principal keystone, carved with the Paschal Lamb, allows a clearer reading of its plan.

Paschal lamb, keystone from the antechurch (Cluny, Musée d'Art et d'Archéologie - Musée Ochier).

Abbot Hugues' hostelry[8]

Abbot Hugues' hostelry: south gable and detail of the lion decorating the pediment.

After leaving the antechurch by the south side door[6] and descending along the retaining wall of the Place de l'Abbaye, visitors reach a vast space, once entirely enclosed. It is bordered to the west by the massive volumes of Abbot Hugues' hostelry on which construction began in 1095.

The lateral face of this building, where windows have been recomposed, housed Napoleon I's stallion shed. It extended beyond the lane which divided it into two unequal sections. The great guest hall on the first storey, reached by side galleries, was about 10-metres high, with open rafters.

On the ground floor, "Abbot Hugues' stables" provided shelter for visitors' mounts. Apart from the remarkable Romanesque roof frame, the south gable, with its masterful, balanced design and pediment decorated with a lion, is noteworthy.

"Palace of Pope Gelasius" [9]

Facing Abbot Hugues' imposing hostelry, the palace (called "that of Pope Gelasius") presents a refined elevation. Only the uppermost storey, displaying two clerestories♦, dates from the years 1300-1330. The first two storeys were completely redesigned in 1873 by Charles-Jean Laisné (architect-pupil of Eugène Emmanuel Viollet-le-Duc) over a single pointed-arched arcade opening onto the square. The clerestorey tracery windows are rare in Cluniac secular architecture. Furthermore, their proportions, outline mouldings and carving are delicate and expressive. Masks decorating the archivolt springers offer a great harmony of features characteristic of the Gothic period.

The palace's façade was embellished by a Louis-XIII door, traditionally said to have been commissioned by Richelieu. It was removed during 19th-century restoration work in order to reestablish a certain style uniformity to the façade. It is now displayed on the floor of the abbey cellarage.

♦***Clerestory:*** *An upper row of more than two bays or windows, separated by simple supports to form a coherent whole.*

Gothic façade of the palace reconstructed in the 19th century.

Capital from the palace façade (Paris, Musée du Louvre).

Richelieu door, reconstruction and drawing by J.-D. Salvèque.

Opposite and right page **Classical cloister,** circa 1750.

Classical cloister[10]

Erected from 1750 onward, the monumental complex comprised a large central cloister built almost exactly on the site of the Romanesque cloister. The elevation of each of the four sides consists of eleven semicircular arches opening onto groin-vaulted arcades and an upper storey, pierced with simple rectangular openings set above each arch. A strongly moulded entablature or coping crowns the composition and supports a roof covered with flat tiles. Its square plan (each side 58 metres across) was occupied, to the north, by the second abbey church, Cluny 2, and to the north, by the Romanesque cloister.

During the years 1120-1130, this latter cloister had been extended over the site of the nave of Cluny 2, demolished after Cluny 3 was built.

The carving on the Pons cloister capitals was extremely lavish, as fragments found on the site attest: elaborate and vigorous foliage, diverse geometric motifs, and the like. Heightened with bright colours, this cloister, whose galleries and central garden provided the setting for the monks' daily existence, was a place both for meditation and intense communal life.

The austere majesty of the Classical architecture which followed it bears witness to the changing concept of the world since Medieval times. The cloister galleries typically gave access to the abbey church: this arrangement, inherited from the Middle Ages, was retained in the new 18th-century plan. Towards the north, the east gallery served the great transept; the north gallery led to the Passage Galilée.

Capitals from the Pons cloister, 12th century, and drawings by Kenneth John Conant (Cluny, Musée d'Art et d'Archéologie - Musée Ochier).

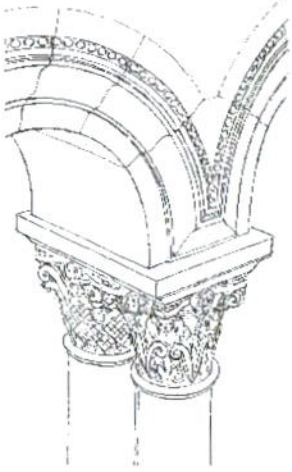

Passage Galilée, leading to a side door of the great church.

Passage Galilée[11]

The name Galilée derives from the porch of the same name at Cluny 2, demolished during the Classical period renovation. The passage or arcade which linked this porch with the nave of Cluny 3 had been maintained. Restored to its early 17th-century appearance, it consists of four groin-vaulted bays with semicircular transverse arches, bonded with small gauged♦ and pricked stones.
The bordering west and east walls display Medieval perforations. The last bay, furthest to the north, rests against the outer gutter wall of the small aisle along the nave through which the Galilée door opens. This relatively low bay partly masks the portal which one notices only upon approaching it. Two Romanesque capitals supporting the archivolt can then be seen above the column shafts.

Towards the east, the north bay leads through a modern passage to the Cour de la Congrégation.

♦***Gauged or tooled:*** *The striated aspect which remains after a stone surface has been dressed with a toothed hammer.*

Cour de la Congrégation

The court is bordered, to the north, by the outer gutter wall of the small aisle and, to the south, by the 18th-century chapel of the Congregation which replaced the Romanesque "abbot's chapel". This is one of the few places at Cluny where the Romanesque building can be perceived almost perfectly, for here there are no ruins to hinder a clear reading of the architectural volumes.

Cour de la Congrégation, wall of the small aisle and south arm of the great transept.

Computer graphics

Our knowledge regarding Cluny relies as much on traditional scholarship as on the most sophisticated modern techniques. In 1989, as part of a television broadcast on the abbey's role in the development of the Germanic Holy Roman Empire, the German television channel TV-ALL. Südwestfunk used computer graphics to reconstruct the lost church of Cluny 3. Exhibited at Cluny, these images gave rise to a symposium organised in collaboration with the Caisse nationale des monuments historiques [French Historical Monuments Agency] where various related experiments were presented and discussed.

Simultaneously, at the Cluny École nationale des arts et métiers, a terminal studies project called on the same techniques and proposed a project in partnership with IBM. In order to recreate the architectural spaces of the great church, engineering students (exactly like the German team) based their measured drawings on the results of excavations and Kenneth John Conant's drawings, as well as measurements of surface features surveyed manually before translation into computerised data. Images obtained were presented to the public in 1992. It is hoped that this new technology, used at Cluny with great demonstrative value, can be applied to future scientific research.

Axonometric view of the chevet of Cluny 3, computer reconstruction IBM Artway.

Great transept[12] of Cluny 3

The transept elevation is crowned by the octagonal "Clocher de l'Eau bénite" ["Holy Water Belfry"]. The skilful distribution of blind arcades and bays, together with richly carved decoration, make it one of the most beautiful of Romanesque towers. It is capped by a slate-covered pyramid whose steeply pitched roof dates from the late 15th century; the cock and fleurs-de-lis cross reach a height of 65 metres. In the 18th century, an additional floor was given to the nearby "Tour de l'Horloge" ["Clock Tower"] to accomodate its clock. This Romanesque tower houses a spiral staircase giving access to the great bell tower and chapel, lit by a rectangular opening, dedicated to the archangel Gabriel. The architectural programme of the abbey church (entirely executed during the Romanesque period) was altogether remarkable. To the rear of the antechurch, the church façade reflected the volumes of the principal nave and its double aisles. Left plain for some years, this façade was perforated with three portals whose central, monumental one was carved abundantly.

The projecting aspect of the portal was reinforced by vivid polychrome carvings: it stood out like an illumination on one of the manuscripts which the abbey *scriptorium*♦ was so adept at producing. From the other side of the great doors, a colossal nave appeared; its 125-metre long perspective was closed by the colonnade and half-cupola of the wide apse, decorated with wall paintings depicting Christ in Glory and symbols of the four evangelists against a gold background. The divine figure seemed to float in the light from the eleven sanctuary windows, a vision intensified at sunrise.

Left page
Great transept, 11th century.

"Holy Water Belfry" gemel bay, 12th century.

♦Scriptorium: *A room reserved for the art of writing and illumination.*

Below
Great nave at Cluny, wash drawing attributed to Jean-Baptiste Lallemand, circa 1770, (private collection).

Tympanum eagle from Cluny 3 (Paris, Musée du Louvre).

Ruins of Cluny 3, lithograph by Émile Sagot, 19th century (private collection).

♦*Apsidiole:* *A small, projecting choir or apse chapel.*

The nave, whose slightly pointed, curved vault soared 30 metres high, extended along 75 metres. Its elevation combined strength and elegance in a subtle play on tiered vertical supports and strongly projecting cornices accentuating the three storeys. The aisles (respectively 17 and 10 metres high) as well as the two transepts with their strongly projecting arms as supports for cupolas and bell towers, provided opportunities for numerous perspectives. Many chapels or apsidioles♦ opened from the east side of these transept arms; they played a role in the overall aspect of the chevet.

By means of its graceful marble colonnade, the great apse communicated with the

Deambulatory of Cluny 3, drawing by Jean-Baptiste Lallemand, 18th century (Paris, Bibliothèque nationale de France).

ambulatory and its five radiating chapels. Its capitals have been preserved, presented in the flour store. Cluniac Romanesque architecture promoted the role of light which flooded the interior volumes through the three hundred and one windows, artfully distributed due to the tiered arrangement of the chevet, transept arms and aisles.

The building has unfortunately almost totally disappeared. All that remains is the south arm of the great transept whose elevation now towers amongst other more ruined parts. From the Cour de la Congrégation, on the other side of the transept door, the impression of weightlessness of interior volumes creates a striking contrast with the exterior.

The octagonal cupola rose to a height of 31.5 metres borne by the great pointed arches springing from the baskets of the Corinthian capitals supported by engaged columns which rose without a break from ground level. These vaults, the highest Romanesque vaulting in the world, repudiated all characteristics normally defining Romanesque architecture. Only three bays of this transept have survived, onto which a Romanesque apsidiole (consecrated to Saint Stephen) opens to the south, and a collapsed Gothic chapel, built from 1330 by Abbot Pierre de Chastelus and dedicated to Saint Martial. The arm has been isolated from the north void by some mediocre masonry erected after demolition work, marking off an area which became the chapel of the school installed in the monastic buildings after 1866.

The small aisle which crossed the south arm has partially survived: one west bay remains, while two east bays separating the two transepts are in ruins. These led to the small transept where the Romanesque chapel apsidiole dedicated to Saint Léger stands next to the portal into Jean de Bourbon's chapel.

Small aisle, drawing by Balthazar Hubert de Saint-Didier, early 19th century (private collection).

Capital with monkeys from the great transept.

Jean de Bourbon's chapel [14]

Work began in 1460 to built this chapel against the east wall of the small transept to replace a small Romanesque apsidiole dedicated to Saint Eutropius. Commissioned by Abbot Jean de Bourbon, it was used as a private and funerary chapel. A small adjacent oratory, fitted with a chimneypiece, allowed him to follow divine office in comfort, out of sight.

Jean de Bourbon's chapel, apse *(top left)*, canopy *(top right)*, King David console *(above)*, lithograph *(bottom)* by Émile Sagot, 19th century (private collection).

Liturgical piscina: *A stone basin set in a niche near the altar used by the priest for draining the wine and water of the Mass and for rinsing Communion vessels.*

The chapel's magnificent decor is still perceptible despite damage inflicted during the Wars of Religion. It consists of two straight bays and a three-sided apse with cross-ribbed vaulting. While its dimensions are modest (11.5 metres long by 5 metres wide), its ashlar masonry is of remarkably high quality. Its iconographic programme presents the Old and New Testaments. Fifteen prophets sculpted into consoles support niches crowned with canopies and pinnacles which held life-size statues of the apostles, Saint John the Baptist and the Virgin Mary.

A liturgical piscina♦ completes the arrangement. The keystones bear the arms of the abbey (Saint Peter's keys and Saint Paul's sword, Cluny's two patron saints), the abbot and his Puy-en-Velay diocese. All this polychromatic, gilded, sculpted decoration was further enhanced by coloured light admitted by the stained-glass windows and the richness of the altar and its painted retable, complemented by the tomb and gisant [recumbent effigy] of its founder. This precious setting is representative of the aesthetics fashionable with influential personages during the 15th century, particularly at the Court of Burgundy. The style of the prophet consoles can be compared with the best work of major sculptors working for the Duke of Burgundy.

Cellarage,
Gothic vaults.

Cellarage and flour store[16]

To the south-east of the park stands a late 13th-century Gothic building, one of the rare edifices remaining from the Medieval abbey. Although reduced lengthwise during the 18th-century building campaign (it now measures 36 metres by 12 metres), it constitutes (in association with the Tour du Moulin with which it communicates) a design group of great significance. Its partially subterranean first level, called the cellarage or store-room, is divided into two equal naves whose vaults rest on a row of octagonal-section columns.
The architecture is sober but elegant: volumentric proportions, soaring columns and profiles of vaults on intersecting semicircular arches contribute fully to this effect. The store-room was lit by small, high bay windows, but most were modified in the 19th century and enlarged. An arm of the mill-race called "des Quatre Moulins [Four Mills]" used to traverse the room, the latter reached through two large side doors. These various arrangements confirm one of its uses, connected with the storage of wine.
The second level is covered by a barrel-vault frame whose chevron-pattern structure forming a truss♦ is characteristic of the Gothic art of carpentry. Made of oak, it has only undergone a little early 20th-century restoration work, consisting of the installation of a wind brace♦ above the tie beam♦. This operation was signed by the *"compagnons du devoir"* [a guild of carpenter-journeymen] who deposited a crucifix and

♦***Truss:***
A rigid framework of timbers placed laterally across the building to carry the longitudinal roof timbers which support the common rafters.

♦***Wind brace:***
Subsidiary timbers set diagonally to strengthen the roof frame.

♦***Tie beam:***
The main horizontal transverse timber of a roof frame.

The 18th-century monastic buildings [15]

Moving from the chapel chevet towards the east gardens, visitors discover the Classical façades of the monastic buildings. These are arranged in a U-shaped plan around a garden whose flower beds were formerly planted with boxwood and cordoned apple-trees. The essential ornamentation is focused on the central avant-corps, or projecting pavilion, and on the two side-wing façades crowned with triangular pediments. The sculpture on the central pediment, unfortunately roughly hacked away, represented the abbey's coat of arms framed with rocaille♦, executed by the same craftsman as the ornamental clasps♦ embellishing the curved lintels of the bay windows. The highly repetitive rhythm of windows on the other façades would be monotonous but for the vigorous profiles of string courses and cornices accentuating the storeys. The most striking decorative effect is provided by the painted and gilded wrought-iron balcony balustrades which contribute to ennobling this otherwise strict composition. Work of a prodigiously prolific blacksmith called Brother Placide (whose real name was Jean Julien), these balustrades, together with the banisters of the monumental staircases leading to the first floor of the monastic buildings, number amongst his most beautiful achievements.

Monastic buildings, façade over looking the park, 18th century *(above)* and ground floor of the central pavilion *(opposite)*.

The first-storey plan is organised around large galleries, with groin vaults on traverse arches, which serve the monks' bedrooms on either side. A vast central vestibule opens onto a balcony through three French windows overlooking the park. This arrangement is also found, simplified, on the façades of the wings.
The programme of this Classical ensemble is simple and functional for the monks' cells, but very extravagant for the horizontal and vertical circulation systems. The design is inspired from the architecture of secular administrative buildings.

♦Rocaille: *An 18th-century ornamental style based on rock and shell motifs.*

♦Clasp: *A projecting keystone of a vaulted opening carrying a sculpted motif.*

Clasp in the rocaille style.

Roof frame of the flour store, circa 1275.

rosary accompanied by the following inscription: *"Un travail pénible et dangereux devient facile et agréable sous le regard de Dieu"* ["Hard and dangerous work becomes easy and agreeable beneath the watch of God"]. The room is amply lit by simple window bays on the south side and by double bays with window seats to the north. A conduit set in the south-east corner suggests that grain was stored there and poured out towards the tower mill. The use of this room as a flour store remains hypothetical but the absence of any chimney-pieces or panelling under the roof frame renders it difficult to envisage any domestic use. Since 1950, the room has been used as an exhibition gallery. Several scale models are displayed there, executed by G. Latapie based on the work of the American archaeologist K. J. Conant, as well as one made in 1855 by François Gueugnon, a Cluny resident. The eight, 80-centimetre high capitals from the round end of the Cluny 3 choir are situated here, each presented on a marble drum from the choir colonnade.

Choir of Cluny 3, model by G. Latapie, after Kenneth John Conant.

Their overall iconographic programme remains difficult to interpret, and their dates imprecise. The main themes are the seasons, the *palaestra*♦, the four winds, the theological virtues, the four trees and four rivers of Paradise, and the eight plainsong♦ tones. Certain capitals represent Adam and Eve, the sacrifice of Abraham, and motifs based on acanthus leaves and fantastic animals. This series is accompanied by a marble altar table which also came from Cluny and an urn traditionally said to have contained Saint Hugues' heart.

♦Palaestra: *An exercise ground for athletes, where wrestling was practised.*

♦Plainsong: *Unaccompanied liturgical music sung in unison in Medieval modes and in free rhythm corresponding to the accentuation of the words (also known as Gregorian chant).*

Choir capitals at Cluny, left to right: bee-keeper, tintinabulum ("tinkling bell"), third plainsong tone, trees of paradise (fig and apple), charity.

A short bibliography

Erlande-Brandenburg (Alain),
L'Abbaye de Cluny,
Rennes, Éditions Ouest-France and Paris, CNMHS, 1993.

Garrigou Grandchamp (Pierre) *et al.*,
La Ville de Cluny et ses maisons (XIe-XVe siècles),
Paris, Éditions Picard, 1997.

Le Gouvernement d'Hugues de Semur à Cluny, Actes du colloque scientifique international, Cluny, September 1988, Cluny, Ville de Cluny and Musée Ochier, 1990.

Iogna-Prat (Dominique),
« Cluny à la mort de saint Maïeul (994-998) »,
Bulletin de la Société de fouilles archéologiques et des monuments historiques de l'Yonne, vol. 12, 1995.

Marguery-Melin (Bruno),
La Destruction de l'abbaye de Cluny 1789-1823,
Cluny, Centre d'études clunisiennes, 1985.

Maurice (Brigitte) et Salvèque (Jean-Denis),
Cluny III. La maior ecclesia,
Cluny, Musée Ochier and Centre d'études clunisiennes, 1988.

Stratford (Neil),
« Les bâtiments de l'abbaye de Cluny à l'époque médiévale. État des questions »,
Bulletin monumental,
vol. 150, 1992, pp. 383-411.

Vingtain (Dominique),
L'Abbaye de Cluny,
Paris, joint publication, Éditions du patrimoine/CNRS Éditions, « Patrimoine au présent » collection, 1998.

CMN : Centre des monuments nationaux, Paris.
MAP,AP : Médiathèque de l'architecture et du patrimoine, Archives photographiques, Paris.

Captions

Cover

Front: Clocher de l'Eau bénite and, in the foreground, Tour des Fromages.
Back: Capital from the choir, Cluny 3 (Charity).
Front flap: "Palace of Pope Gelasius", lithograph by Émile Sagot, private collection.
Back flap: Detail from the Saint-Martin-des-Champs manuscript, Paris, BnF.

Visit, p. 38:
Palace of Jacques d'Amboise, detail of the alabaster decor.

Chronology

Left to right and top to bottom:
•Politics and religion: Monastery of Paray-le-Monial, CMN/René-Jacques; detail of the Koran, see p. 19; Cardinal Richelieu, see p. 23.
•Cluniac history: Gunzo relates his vision to Abbot Hugues (detail), see p. 9; Cardinal Bouillon, see p. 23; Cardinal de La Rochefoucauld, see p. 24.
•The abbey: consecration of an altar at Cluny by Urban II (detail), see p. 11; roof frame of the flour store, see p. 63; "Richelieu door", see p. 51; central pavilion ground floor of the monastic buildings, see p. 61; Kenneth John Conant, see p. 30.
•Religious architecture: Avignon, Papal palace, CMN/É. Revault; Paris, Abbey of Val-de-Grâce, CMN/P. Lemaître; Jumièges, ruined church of Saint Peter, CMN/C. Rose; Vézelay, interior of the basilica, CMN/A. Lonchampt.

Photographic credits

Asb Baudat Bensheim: p. 12; BnF: back flap, p. 5, 7, 9, 10-11, 19b, 47t, 59t; Cluny, Musée d'Art et d'Archéologie (Musée Ochier): p. 1c, 1b, 8, 14-15t, 14b, 23b, 24, 28b, 29, 30, 34t, 37t, 45tl, 45tr, 47c, 52bl, 52br; CMN/P. Berthé: p. 60b; CMN/D. Bordes: back cover, p. 38-41, 42t, 42br, 42bl, 46, 54t, 60tl, 60c, 62t, 62b, 63b; CMN/P. Cadet: p. 17t, 58; CMN/René- Jacques: p. 17br; CMN/É. Revault: p. 20t; CMN/M. Tulane: p. 20b; DR: p. 22t, 57b; Éditions Complexe: p. 25; Explorer/P. Wisocky: p. 51t; Giraudon: p. 18t, 23tl, 23tr; Hoa Qui: front cover, p. 19t; IBM/Artway: p. 55; Jean-Denis Salvèque, Centre d'études clunisiennes: p. 1t, 4, 6t, 13, 15b, 16t, 16b, 17bl, 21, 22b, 26-27, 31, 32-33, 34b, 35, 37b, 43, 45b, 48-50, 51b, 52t, 53, 54b, 56, 57t, 59c, 59b, 60tr, 61t, 61c, 61b, 63t; Le Journal de Saône-et-Loire/L'Europe vue du ciel: p. 2-3; Michel Bouillot, Centre d'études clunisiennes: p. 44b; MAP, AP: p. 28t, 36, 47b, 63c; RMN: p. 44t; RMN/Chuzeville: p. 51c; RMN/Lewandowski: p. 57c; Ville de Souvigny: p. 6b.

Collection director
Alix Sallé
Editorial coordinator
Chloé Demey
Documentation coordinator
Alice Perrin
Translator
Ann Sautier-Greening
Copy editor
Barbara Shapiro Comte
Graphic design
Atalante/Paris
Layout
encore/Paris
Computer graphics
Jean-Denis Salvèque and Jean-Philippe Guillerme
(back cover)
Production coordinator
Carine Merse
Photoengraving
Quattro/Cuincy
Printing
Néo-Typo/Besançon, France

Dépôt légal: May 2001
Reprinting: July 2005